FROM ENGINEER TO LEADER

A GUIDE TO ACHIEVING SUCCESS IN ENGINEERING MANAGEMENT

SUMON MAL

This book is dedicated to all the engineers who strive to make a difference in their field, and to the managers who lead them.

Engineering management is a challenging field, but it is also one that is filled with opportunities to make a positive impact on the world. It takes dedication, hard work, and a commitment to excellence to be a successful engineering manager.

This book is a tribute to all the engineers and managers who have dedicated their lives to this field, and who continue to push the boundaries of what is possible. It is a reminder of the importance of the work that we do and the difference that we can make.

I hope that this book will serve as a valuable resource for those who are just starting their careers in engineering management, as well as for those who are seasoned professionals. May it inspire and guide you as you navigate the field of engineering management.

Sumon Mal

Contents

Contents

FOREWORD

Engineering management is a vital field that plays an important role in the success of any engineering project. As an engineering manager, you must be able to lead teams of engineers, manage projects, and make important decisions that affect the outcome of your projects. The role of an engineering manager is critical to the success of any engineering project, and the skills and knowledge that you possess can make or break the project.

This book is an essential resource for anyone seeking to understand the principles of engineering management and the skills necessary to be a successful engineering manager. It covers key concepts such as understanding the software engineering industry, developing technical skills, leadership and communication, software project management, financial management, problem solving and decision making, time management and prioritization, mentorship and networking, business acumen, technical acumen, people growth, process management, risk management, change management, scope management, priority management, learning and development, people/team performance management, team appraisal management, team conflict handling and dealing with empathy.

The book is written in a clear and concise manner, making it easy to understand even for those with little or no background in engineering management. The author has provided practical tips and strategies for developing the skills necessary for success in engineering management, making it a valuable resource for both new and experienced engineering managers alike.

If you are looking to advance your career in engineering management or are simply interested in learning more about the field, this book is an essential read. It is packed with valuable information and insights that will help you become a successful engineering manager and lead your teams to success.

I highly recommend this book to anyone looking to understand the principles of engineering management and the skills necessary to be a successful engineering manager. It is a must-read for anyone seeking to advance their career in this field.

Sumon Mal

Preface

Engineering management is a field that is vital to the success of any engineering project. As an engineering manager, you are responsible for leading teams of engineers, managing projects, and making important decisions that affect the outcome of your projects. This book is written to provide an overview of the key concepts and skills necessary for success in engineering management.

This book is designed to help readers understand the principles of engineering management and the skills necessary to be a successful engineering manager. We will explore the software engineering industry, the technical skills required for success in the field, leadership and communication, software project management, financial management, problem solving and decision making, time management and prioritization, mentorship and networking, business acumen, technical acumen, people growth, process management, risk management, change management, scope management, priority management, learning and development, people/team performance management, team appraisal management, team conflict handling, and dealing with empathy.

This book is written for anyone who is interested in understanding the principles of engineering management and the skills necessary to be a successful engineering manager. Whether you are just starting your career in engineering management or are a seasoned professional, this book provides valuable insights and information that can help you advance in your career and become a successful engineering manager.

I have tried to make this book as informative and practical as possible, with examples and case studies that illustrate the key concepts discussed in each chapter. We have also included tips and strategies for developing the skills necessary for success in engineering management, making it a valuable resource for both new and experienced engineering managers alike.

I hope that this book will be a valuable resource for anyone seeking to understand the principles of engineering management and the skills necessary to be a successful engineering manager.

Sumon Mal

Acknowledgements

Writing a book is a significant undertaking, and I would like to take this opportunity to thank all those who have helped me in the process.

I would like to express my gratitude to my mentor who provided me with invaluable guidance, support, and encouragement throughout the entire process. Their wisdom, experience, and expertise have been instrumental in shaping this book and making it a reality.

I would also like to thank my colleagues and friends who provided me with feedback, support, and encouragement. Their contributions, whether big or small, have been invaluable and have helped me to improve this book.

I am also grateful to the team who helped me with the editing, formatting, and publishing process. Their support and expertise have been instrumental in bringing this book to fruition.

Finally, I would like to thank my family for their unwavering support, encouragement, and love. Their understanding and patience have been essential in allowing me to complete this book.

I am grateful to all those who have helped me in this journey, and I hope that this book will be of value to readers.

Sumon Mal

PROLOGUE

Welcome to this book on engineering management. As you embark on this journey, you will learn about the key concepts and skills necessary for success in this field. Engineering management is a vital field that plays an important role in the success of any engineering project. As an engineering manager, you must be able to lead teams of engineers, manage projects, and make important decisions that affect the outcome of your projects.

This book is written to provide an overview of the key concepts and skills necessary for success in engineering management. We will explore the software engineering industry, the technical skills required for success in the field, leadership and communication, software project management, financial management, problem solving and decision making, time management and prioritization, mentorship and networking, business acumen, technical acumen, people growth, process management, risk management, change management, scope management, priority management, learning and development, people/team performance management, team appraisal management, team conflict handling, and dealing with empathy.

As you read through each chapter, you will gain a deeper understanding of the field of engineering management and the skills necessary to be a successful engineering manager. You will also learn about the challenges and opportunities that come with being an engineering manager, and gain insights on how to navigate them.

This book is written for anyone who is interested in understanding the principles of engineering management and the skills necessary to be a successful engineering manager. Whether you are just starting your career in engineering management or are a seasoned professional, this book provides valuable insights and information that can help you advance in your career and become a successful engineering manager.

As you read through this book, take note of the key concepts, and try to apply them to your own work as an engineering manager. We hope that this book will be a valuable resource for you as you navigate the field of engineering management.

Let's begin this journey, and discover the world of engineering management together.

I

Introduction to Engineering Management

Engineering management is the application of engineering principles and practices to the management of organizations. It is a critical field that is responsible for the planning, coordination, and control of technical and engineering projects. As an engineering manager, you will be responsible for leading teams of engineers and ensuring that projects are completed on time, within budget, and to the required quality standards.

This book is designed to provide an overview of the key concepts and skills necessary for success in engineering management. We will explore the software engineering industry, the technical skills required for success in the field, leadership and communication, software project management, financial management, problem solving and decision making, time management and prioritization, mentorship and networking, business acumen, technical acumen, people growth, process management, risk management, change management, scope management, priority management, learning and development, people/team performance management, team appraisal management, team conflict handling and dealing with empathy.

Throughout this book, we will provide tips and strategies for developing the skills necessary for success in engineering management. We will start by understanding the software engineering industry and the technical skills required for success in the field, as discussed in Chapter 2. We will then delve into the importance of leadership and communication, as outlined in Chapter 4, and learn about the key principles of software project management in Chapter 5. We will also explore the financial management strategies, as discussed in Chapter 6, and the importance of problem-solving and decision-making, as outlined in Chapter 7. We will delve into the importance of time management and prioritization, as discussed in Chapter 8, and the role of mentorship and networking, as outlined in Chapter 9. We will also learn about the business acumen, technical acumen, people growth, and process management, as discussed in Chapter 10,11,12,13 respectively. We will also explore the key concepts of risk management, change management, scope management, and priority management, as discussed in Chapter 14,15,16,17 respectively. We will delve into the importance of learning and development, as discussed in Chapter 18, and the people/team performance management, team appraisal management, team conflict handling and dealing with empathy, as outlined in Chapter 19,20,21,22 respectively.

Whether you are just starting your career in engineering management or are a seasoned professional

In conclusion, engineering management is a challenging and rewarding field that requires a combination of technical, business, and leadership skills. It is a field that is constantly evolving, and engineering managers must be committed to ongoing learning and development in order to stay current and be successful.

II

Understanding the Software Engineering Industry

The software engineering industry is a rapidly growing field that plays a critical role in today's digital world. Software engineers are responsible for designing, developing, testing, and maintaining software systems that are used in a wide range of industries, including technology, finance, healthcare, transportation, and more. In this chapter, we will explore the software engineering industry in more detail, including its history, current trends, and challenges.

The history of software engineering can be traced back to the 1950s, when the first computers were developed. At that time, software engineering was primarily focused on developing software for scientific and military applications.

However, as computers became more prevalent in society, the field of software engineering began to expand. In the 1960s, software engineering began to focus on developing software for business applications, such as accounting and inventory management.

In the 1970s, the software engineering industry began to focus on developing software for personal computers. This was a major turning point in the industry, as it allowed software engineers to develop applications that were accessible to a wider audience. In the 1980s, the software engineering industry began to focus on developing software for the internet. This was a significant development, as it allowed software engineers to develop applications that could be used by people all over the world.

Today, the software engineering industry is a rapidly growing field that plays a critical role in the digital world. The industry is driven by the increasing use of technology in society, as well as the growing demand for software applications in a wide range of industries. The software engineering industry is also driven by the increasing use of mobile devices, such as smartphones and tablets, as well as the growing use of the internet and cloud computing.

Current trends in the software engineering industry include the increasing use of Agile development methodologies, the growing use of machine learning and artificial intelligence, and the increasing use of open-source software. Agile development methodologies are a set of practices that are designed to help software engineers develop software more quickly and efficiently. Machine learning and artificial intelligence are technologies that are being used to develop software that can learn and adapt to changing conditions. Open-source software is software that is available to the public for free, and it is becoming increasingly popular in the software engineering industry.

Challenges facing the software engineering industry include the growing demand for software engineers, the increasing complexity of software systems, and the need to stay current with new technologies and industry developments. The demand for software engineers is growing faster than the supply, which has led to a shortage of qualified software engineers. The increasing complexity of software systems has made it more challenging for software engineers to develop software that is reliable, efficient, and easy to use. Additionally, software engineers must stay current with new technologies and industry developments in order to be competitive in the industry.

In conclusion, the software engineering industry is a rapidly growing field that plays a critical role in today's digital world. The industry is driven by the increasing use of technology in society, as well as the growing demand for software applications in a wide range of industries. Current trends in the software engineering industry include the increasing use of Agile development methodologies, the growing use of machine learning and artificial intelligence, and the increasing use of open-source software. Challenges facing the software engineering industry include the growing demand for software engineers, the increasing complexity of software systems, and the need to stay current with new technologies and industry developments. To succeed in this field, software engineers must be committed to ongoing learning and development, and be able to adapt to changing industry trends.

III

Developing Technical Skills

As a software engineer, it is essential to have a strong foundation in the technical skills necessary to design, develop, test, and maintain software systems. In this chapter, we will explore the technical skills that are essential for success in the software industry and how to develop and maintain them.

One of the most important technical skills for software engineers is the ability to code. This includes knowledge of programming languages such as Java, C++, Python, and JavaScript. It is also essential to have a good understanding of data structures, algorithms, and software design patterns. These skills are essential for writing efficient and maintainable code, as well as for troubleshooting and debugging software systems.

Another important technical skill for software engineers is the ability to work with databases. This includes knowledge of database management systems such as MySQL, Oracle, and SQL Server, as well as the ability to write SQL queries and perform data modeling. These skills are essential for managing and manipulating data in software systems.

In addition to coding and database management, software engineers must also have a good understanding of software testing and quality assurance. This includes knowledge of testing methods such as unit testing, integration testing, and acceptance testing, as well as the ability to write test cases and test plans. These skills are essential for ensuring that software systems are reliable and free of defects.

Another important technical skill for software engineers is the ability to work with version control systems such as Git, Mercurial, and Subversion. These tools are used to manage and track changes to software systems and are essential for collaboration and teamwork. Software engineers must also be familiar with software development methodologies such as Agile and Scrum, as well as project management tools such as JIRA, Trello, and Asana.

To develop and maintain technical skills in the software industry, it is essential to stay current with new technologies and industry developments. This can be achieved through continuous learning, such as taking online courses, attending conferences and workshops, and reading industry publications. It is also important to work on real-world projects, as this provides hands-on experience and the opportunity to apply the skills learned in a practical setting.

Networking with other software engineers is also an important way to develop and maintain technical skills. This can be achieved through online forums, social media, and professional organizations. Joining a team of software engineers or starting your own software development project can also provide valuable experience and opportunities to learn from others.

Finally, it is important to seek mentorship from experienced software engineers. This can provide guidance and support, as well as the opportunity to learn from those who have successfully navigated the challenges of the software industry.

In conclusion, having a strong foundation in technical skills is essential for success in the software industry. These skills include coding, database management, software testing and quality assurance, version control, and software development methodologies. To develop and maintain these skills, it is essential to stay current with new technologies and industry developments, network with other software engineers, work on real-world projects, and seek mentorship from experienced software engineers. By investing in your technical skills, you can build a successful career in the software industry.

IV

Leadership and Communication

Leadership and communication are critical skills for engineering managers. They play a crucial role in guiding and motivating teams, building relationships with stakeholders, and making strategic decisions that drive the success of engineering projects and organizations. In this chapter, we will explore the role of leadership and communication in engineering management and provide tips for effective leadership and communication in the engineering industry.

Leadership is the ability to inspire and guide teams to achieve common goals. As an engineering manager, you must be able to lead by example and inspire your team to work together towards a shared vision. This includes setting clear goals, providing guidance and support, and fostering a culture of trust and collaboration. Additionally, you must be able to make difficult decisions, manage conflict, and resolve problems.

Communication is the ability to share information and ideas effectively. As an engineering manager, you must be able to communicate clearly and effectively with your team, stakeholders, and customers. This includes being able to present complex technical information in a way that is easy to understand, as well as being able to listen actively and respond to feedback. Additionally, you must be able to negotiate and persuade others to support your ideas and decisions.

To be an effective leader and communicator in the engineering industry, it is important to develop the following skills:

Active listening: To effectively communicate with others, you must be able to listen actively and understand their perspectives. This includes paying attention to nonverbal cues, asking clarifying questions, and providing feedback.

Empathy: To be an effective leader, you must be able to understand and relate to the emotions and concerns of your team members. This includes being able to provide support and guidance, as well as being able to recognize and address issues that may be affecting team morale.

Conflict resolution: As an engineering manager, you will encounter conflicts and disagreements. To effectively resolve them, you must be able to identify the root cause of the conflict, communicate with all parties involved, and find a solution that is mutually beneficial.

Team building: To be an effective leader, you must be able to build a strong and cohesive team. This includes fostering a culture of trust and collaboration, as well as providing opportunities for team members to develop their skills and advance their careers.

Adaptability: As an engineering manager, you must be able to adapt to changing circumstances and respond to unexpected challenges. This includes being able to pivot your strategy, communicate effectively with your team, and manage change.

In addition to developing the above skills, you must also be able to apply them in a professional setting. This includes being able to communicate effectively with your team and stakeholders, providing guidance and support, and making strategic decisions. Additionally, you must be able to build relationships with customers and other stakeholders, negotiate and persuade others to support your ideas and decisions, and manage conflict and resolve problems.

To be an effective leader and communicator in the engineering industry, it is also important to stay current with new technologies and industry developments. This can be achieved through continuous learning, such as taking online courses, attending conferences and workshops, and reading industry publications. Additionally, networking with other engineering managers and industry professionals can provide valuable opportunities to learn from others and build relationships.

In conclusion, leadership and communication are critical skills for engineering managers. They play a crucial role in guiding and motivating teams, building relationships with stakeholders, and making strategic decisions that drive the success of engineering projects and organizations. To be an effective leader and communicator in the engineering industry, it is important to develop skills such as active listening, empathy, conflict resolution, team building, and adaptability, and stay current with new technologies and industry developments.

V

Business Acumen

Business acumen is the understanding and knowledge of how businesses operate and the ability to make informed and strategic business decisions. In this chapter, we will explore the importance of business acumen in engineering management and provide tips for developing and honing business acumen skills in the engineering industry.

The importance of business acumen in engineering management lies in the ability to understand and navigate the business aspects of the engineering industry. This includes understanding financial statements, budgeting and forecasting, and identifying and managing risks. Additionally, engineering managers must be able to make informed and strategic business decisions that align with the organization's overall goals and objectives.

Effective business acumen in the engineering industry requires a combination of technical, business, and leadership skills. Technical skills include knowledge of engineering principles and practices, as well as problem-solving techniques. Business skills include knowledge of finance, accounting, and marketing. Leadership skills include the ability to inspire and motivate teams, make difficult decisions, and resolve problems.

To develop and hone business acumen skills in the engineering industry, it is important to:

Continuously learn and stay current with industry trends and developments

Develop a strong understanding of financial statements and budgeting

Network with industry professionals and executives

Seek out opportunities to take on business-related responsibilities within your organization

Attend industry conferences and events to learn about the latest trends and best practices

In addition to developing the above skills, it is also important to apply them in a professional setting. This includes being able to understand and navigate the business aspects of the engineering industry, make informed and strategic business decisions, and communicate effectively with stakeholders and customers. By developing and honing business acumen skills, you can become a valuable asset to your organization and advance in your career as an engineering manager.

VI

Technical Acumen

Technical acumen is the understanding and knowledge of engineering principles and practices and the ability to apply them in a professional setting. In this chapter, we will explore the importance of technical acumen in engineering management and provide tips for developing and honing technical acumen skills in the engineering industry.

The importance of technical acumen in engineering management lies in the ability to understand and navigate the technical aspects of the engineering industry. This includes understanding and applying engineering principles, design processes, and problem-solving techniques. Additionally, engineering managers must be able to make informed and strategic technical decisions that align with the organization's overall goals and objectives.

Effective technical acumen in the engineering industry requires a combination of technical, business, and leadership skills. Technical skills include knowledge of engineering principles and practices, as well as programming languages and tools. Business skills include knowledge of project management methodologies and decision-making frameworks. Leadership skills include the ability to inspire and motivate teams, make difficult decisions, and resolve problems.

To develop and hone technical acumen skills in the engineering industry, it is important to:

Continuously learn and stay current with industry trends and developments: This includes taking courses and attending workshops to stay up to date with the latest technologies and best practices.

Develop a strong understanding of engineering principles and practices: This includes understanding the design process, problem-solving techniques, and the use of programming languages and tools.

Network with industry professionals and experts: This includes joining professional organizations and attending industry events to connect with other professionals and learn from experts in the field.

Seek out opportunities to take on technical responsibilities within your organization: This includes leading technical projects and mentoring junior engineers.

Practice and apply your technical skills in a professional setting: This includes working on real-world projects and applying your skills to solve real-world problems.

In addition to developing the above skills, it is also important to apply them in a professional setting. This includes being able to understand and navigate the technical aspects of the engineering industry, make informed and strategic technical decisions, and communicate effectively with technical team members. By developing and honing technical acumen skills, you can become a valuable asset to your organization and advance in your career as an engineering manager.

VII

People Growth

People growth is the ability to lead, motivate, and develop a team to achieve their full potential. In this chapter, we will explore the importance of people growth in engineering management and provide tips for developing and honing people growth skills in the engineering industry.

The importance of people growth in engineering management lies in the ability to lead and motivate a team to achieve their full potential. This includes understanding and managing the needs of team members, providing clear direction and guidance, and fostering a positive and productive work environment. Additionally, engineering managers must be able to identify and develop the skills and talents of team members to ensure that the team is able to meet the goals and objectives of the organization.

Effective people growth in the engineering industry requires a combination of technical, business, and leadership skills. Technical skills include knowledge of engineering principles and practices, as well as programming languages and tools. Business skills include knowledge of project management methodologies and decision-making frameworks. Leadership skills include the ability to inspire and motivate teams, make difficult decisions, and resolve problems.

To develop and hone people growth skills in the engineering industry, it is important to:

Understand and manage the needs of team members: This includes understanding the strengths and weaknesses of each team member and providing the support and resources they need to succeed.

Provide clear direction and guidance: This includes setting clear goals and objectives, providing regular feedback, and addressing any issues or concerns that arise.

Foster a positive and productive work environment: This includes creating a culture of open communication, collaboration, and respect.

Identify and develop the skills and talents of team members: This includes providing opportunities for training and development and identifying potential leaders within the team.

Lead by example: This includes setting an example of positive and professional behavior and leading by example in terms of technical and business skills.

In addition to developing the above skills, it is also important to apply them in a professional setting. This includes being able to lead and motivate a team to achieve their full potential, identify and develop the skills and talents of team members, and create a positive and productive work environment. By developing and honing people growth skills, you can become a valuable asset to your organization and advance in your career as an engineering manager.

VIII

Process Management

Process management is the ability to design, implement, and improve processes to increase efficiency and effectiveness. In this chapter, we will explore the importance of process management in engineering management and provide tips for developing and honing process management skills in the engineering industry.

The importance of process management in engineering management lies in the ability to design and implement efficient and effective processes to increase productivity and reduce costs. This includes understanding and applying process management methodologies, such as Six Sigma and Lean, and identifying and addressing bottlenecks and inefficiencies. Additionally, engineering managers must be able to continuously improve processes to stay ahead of the competition and meet the ever-changing needs of the industry.

Effective process management in the engineering industry requires a combination of technical, business, and leadership skills. Technical skills include knowledge of engineering principles and practices, as well as programming languages and tools. Business skills include knowledge of project management methodologies and decision-making frameworks. Leadership skills include the ability to inspire and motivate teams, make difficult decisions, and resolve problems.

To develop and hone process management skills in the engineering industry, it is important to:

Understand and apply process management methodologies: This includes understanding and applying methodologies such as Six Sigma and Lean to design and implement efficient and effective processes.

Identify and address bottlenecks and inefficiencies: This includes using data and metrics to identify and address areas of inefficiency and improve overall productivity.

Continuously improve processes: This includes staying current with industry trends and developments and continuously seeking out new and innovative ways to improve processes.

Collaborate with team members and improve processes.

Continuously improve processes: This includes staying current with industry trends and developments, and implementing new technologies and best practices to improve processes and stay ahead of the competition.

Communicate and collaborate with team members: This includes involving team members in the process design and implementation, and ensuring that they understand the processes and their roles in them.

Measure and track process performance: This includes tracking key performance indicators and using data and metrics to measure the performance of processes and identify areas for improvement.

In addition to developing the above skills, it is also important to apply them in a professional setting. This includes being able to design and implement efficient and effective processes, identify and address bottlenecks and inefficiencies, and continuously improve processes. By developing and honing process management skills, you can become a valuable asset to your organization and advance in your career as an engineering manager.

In conclusion, process management is a critical skill for engineering managers. It involves designing, implementing, and improving processes to increase efficiency and effectiveness. To be an effective process manager in the engineering industry, it is important to understand and apply process management methodologies, identify and address bottlenecks and inefficiencies, continuously improve processes, communicate and collaborate with team members, and measure and track process performance. By developing and honing process management skills, you can become a valuable asset to your organization and advance in your career as an engineering manager.

IX

Financial Management

Financial management is a critical skill for engineering managers, as it involves managing the financial aspects of engineering projects and organizations. This includes budgeting, forecasting, and monitoring costs, as well as making financial decisions that are in the best interest of the organization. In this chapter, we will explore the role of financial management in engineering management and provide tips for effective financial management in the engineering industry.

The role of financial management in engineering management is to provide a framework for managing the financial aspects of engineering projects and organizations. This includes developing budgets, forecasting revenue and expenses, and monitoring costs. Financial managers are also responsible for interpreting financial statements, making financial decisions, and managing the organization's cash flow. Additionally, they must be able to communicate effectively with stakeholders and customers to ensure that the project is meeting their needs.

Effective financial management in the engineering industry requires a combination of technical, business, and leadership skills. Technical skills include knowledge of accounting, financial analysis, and financial modeling. Business skills include knowledge of budgeting, forecasting, and financial management methodologies. Leadership skills include the ability to inspire and motivate teams, make difficult decisions, and resolve problems.

To be an effective financial manager in the engineering industry, it is important to develop the following skills:

Budgeting and forecasting: To effectively manage the financial aspects of engineering projects and organizations, you must be able to develop budgets, forecast revenue and expenses, and monitor costs. This includes analyzing financial statements, interpreting financial data, and identifying potential financial risks and opportunities.

Cost management: As a financial manager, you must be able to effectively manage costs. This includes identifying and controlling costs, as well as monitoring and analyzing variances between actual and budgeted costs.

Financial analysis: To make informed financial decisions, you must be able to analyze and interpret financial data. This includes understanding financial statements, such as income statements, balance sheets, and cash flow statements, as well as performing ratio analysis and cost-benefit analysis.

Risk management: As a financial manager, you must be able to anticipate and manage financial risks. This includes identifying potential financial problems, developing strategies to mitigate risks, and monitoring progress.

Strategic planning: To be an effective financial manager, you must be able to develop and implement financial strategies that align with the organization's overall goals and objectives. This includes identifying and pursuing new revenue streams, as well as managing costs and maximizing profitability.

In addition to developing the above skills, it is also important to apply them in a professional setting. This includes being able to manage the financial aspects of engineering projects and organizations effectively, communicate effectively with stakeholders and customers, and make informed financial decisions. Additionally, you must be able to build relationships with customers and other stakeholders, negotiate and persuade others to support your ideas and decisions, and manage conflict and resolve problems.

It is also essential to stay current with new technologies and industry developments related to financial management. This can be achieved through continuous learning, such as taking online courses, attending conferences and workshops, and reading industry publications. Additionally, networking with other financial managers and industry professionals can provide valuable opportunities to learn from others and build relationships.

In conclusion, financial management is a critical skill for engineering managers. It involves managing the financial aspects of engineering projects and organizations, including budgeting, forecasting, and monitoring costs. To be an effective financial manager in the engineering industry, it is important to develop skills such as budgeting and forecasting, cost management, financial analysis, risk management, and strategic planning. Additionally, it is essential to apply these skills in a professional setting, stay current with new technologies and industry developments, and network with other financial managers and industry professionals. By investing in your financial management skills, you can ensure the financial success of your engineering projects and organization.

X

Project Management

Project management is a critical skill for engineering managers, particularly in the software industry. It involves planning, organizing, and overseeing the execution of software projects to ensure they are completed on time, within budget, and to the required quality standards. In this chapter, we will explore the role of project management in engineering management and provide tips for effective project management in the software industry.

The role of project management in engineering management is to provide a framework for organizing and executing software projects. This includes developing project plans, setting project goals, and identifying and managing project risks. Project managers are also responsible for coordinating the efforts of the project team, including software engineers, designers, and testers. Additionally, they must be able to communicate effectively with stakeholders and customers to ensure that the project is meeting their needs.

Effective project management in the software industry requires a combination of technical, business, and leadership skills. Technical skills include knowledge of software development methodologies such as Agile and Scrum, as well as programming languages and tools such as Java, C++, Python, and JavaScript. Business skills include knowledge of project management methodologies such as PMBOK and PRINCE2, as well as budgeting and financial management. Leadership skills include the ability to inspire and motivate teams, make difficult decisions, and resolve problems.

To be an effective project manager in the software industry, it is important to develop the following skills:

Planning and organizing: To effectively manage software projects, you must be able to plan and organize the project's resources, including personnel, budget, and equipment. This includes developing project plans, setting project goals, and identifying and managing project risks.

Communication: As a project manager, you must be able to communicate effectively with the project team, stakeholders, and customers. This includes being able to present complex technical information in a way that is easy to understand, as well as being able to listen actively and respond to feedback.

Time management: To effectively manage software projects, you must be able to manage your time effectively and meet deadlines. This includes setting priorities, delegating tasks, and monitoring progress.

Risk management: As a project manager, you must be able to anticipate and manage project risks. This includes identifying potential problems, developing strategies to mitigate risks, and monitoring progress.

Adaptability: As a project manager, you must be able to adapt to changing circumstances and respond to unexpected challenges. This includes being able to pivot your strategy, communicate effectively with your team, and manage change.

In addition to developing the above skills, it is also important to apply them in a professional setting. This includes being able to manage software projects effectively, communicate effectively with the project team, stakeholders, and customers, and make strategic decisions. Additionally, you must be able to build relationships with customers and other stakeholders, negotiate and persuade others to support your ideas and decisions, and manage conflict and resolve problems.

XI

Risk Management

Risk management is the process of identifying, assessing, and mitigating potential risks that could impact the success of an engineering project or organization. In this chapter, we will explore the importance of risk management in engineering management and provide tips for developing and implementing effective risk management practices in the engineering industry.

The importance of risk management in engineering management lies in the ability to identify and mitigate potential risks that could impact the success of a project or organization. This includes understanding the types of risks that are relevant to the engineering industry, such as technical risks, financial risks, and organizational risks. Additionally, engineering managers must be able to assess the likelihood and impact of these risks, and implement strategies to mitigate or eliminate them.

Effective risk management in the engineering industry requires a combination of technical, business, and leadership skills. Technical skills include knowledge of engineering principles and practices, as well as problem-solving techniques. Business skills include knowledge of finance, accounting, and project management. Leadership skills include the ability to inspire and motivate teams, make difficult decisions, and resolve problems.

To develop and implement effective risk management practices in the engineering industry, it is important to:

Understand the types of risks that are relevant to the engineering industry: This includes understanding the different types of risks, such as technical risks, financial risks, and organizational risks.

Assess the likelihood and impact of risks: This includes using data and metrics to assess the likelihood and impact of potential risks, and prioritizing them based on their potential impact.

Implement strategies to mitigate or eliminate risks: This includes implementing risk management strategies such as risk avoidance, risk reduction, and risk transfer. This also includes developing risk response plans and contingencies to address potential risks.

Regularly review and update risk management processes: This includes regularly reviewing and updating risk management processes to ensure they are current and effective, and incorporating lessons learned from previous projects.

Communicate and collaborate with team members: This includes involving team members in the risk management process, and ensuring that they understand their roles and responsibilities in identifying and mitigating risks.

Monitor and track risks: This includes regularly monitoring and tracking risks to ensure that they are being effectively managed and that any issues are identified and addressed in a timely manner.

In addition to developing the above skills, it is also important to apply them in a professional setting. This includes being able to identify, assess, and mitigate potential risks that could impact the success of a project or organization. By developing and implementing effective risk management practices, you can become a valuable asset to your organization and advance in your career as an engineering manager.

XII

Change Management

Change management is the process of identifying, assessing, and implementing changes to an engineering project or organization. In this chapter, we will explore the importance of change management in engineering management and provide tips for developing and implementing effective change management practices in the engineering industry.

The importance of change management in engineering management lies in the ability to identify and implement changes to a project or organization that will improve its performance and meet its goals and objectives. This includes understanding the types of changes that are relevant to the engineering industry, such as technical changes, organizational changes, and process changes. Additionally, engineering managers must be able to assess the impact of these changes, and implement strategies to ensure they are successfully implemented.

Effective change management in the engineering industry requires a combination of technical, business, and leadership skills. Technical skills include knowledge of engineering principles and practices, as well as problem-solving techniques. Business skills include knowledge of finance, accounting, and project management. Leadership skills include the ability to inspire and motivate teams, make difficult decisions, and resolve problems.

To develop and implement effective change management practices in the engineering industry, it is important to:

Understand the types of changes that are relevant to the engineering industry: This includes understanding the different types of changes, such as technical changes, organizational changes, and process changes.

Assess the impact of changes: This includes using data and metrics to assess the impact of potential changes, and prioritizing them based on their potential impact.

Implement strategies to ensure changes are successfully implemented: This includes developing change management plans and contingencies, and involving stakeholders in the change management process.

Regularly review and update change management processes: This includes regularly reviewing and updating change management processes to ensure they are current and effective, and incorporating lessons learned from previous projects.

Communicate and collaborate with team members: This includes involving team members in the change management process, and ensuring that they understand their roles and responsibilities in identifying and implementing changes. This also includes communicating the reasons for changes and the expected outcomes to the team and stakeholders.

Monitor and track changes: This includes regularly monitoring and tracking changes to ensure that they are being effectively implemented and that any issues are identified and addressed in a timely manner.

In addition to developing the above skills, it is also important to apply them in a professional setting. This includes being able to identify and implement changes that will improve the performance of a project or organization. By developing and implementing effective change management practices, you can become a valuable asset to your organization and advance in your career as an engineering manager.

XIII

Scope Management

Scope management is the process of identifying, assessing, and controlling the scope of an engineering project or organization. In this chapter, we will explore the importance of scope management in engineering management and provide tips for developing and implementing effective scope management practices in the engineering industry.

The importance of scope management in engineering management lies in the ability to identify and control the scope of a project or organization to ensure that it meets its goals and objectives. This includes understanding the types of scope that are relevant to the engineering industry, such as technical scope, organizational scope, and process scope. Additionally, engineering managers must be able to assess the impact of changes to scope and implement strategies to ensure that scope is effectively managed.

Effective scope management in the engineering industry requires a combination of technical, business, and leadership skills. Technical skills include knowledge of engineering principles and practices, as well as problem-solving techniques. Business skills include knowledge of finance, accounting, and project management. Leadership skills include the ability to inspire and motivate teams, make difficult decisions, and resolve problems.

To develop and implement effective scope management practices in the engineering industry, it is important to:

Understand the types of scope that are relevant to the engineering industry: This includes understanding the different types of scope, such as technical scope, organizational scope, and process scope.

Develop a detailed scope statement: This includes defining and documenting the objectives, deliverables, and constraints of a project.

Establish a scope management plan: This includes outlining the procedures and processes for managing scope, and assigning roles and responsibilities for scope management.

Continuously monitor and control scope: This includes regularly reviewing and updating the scope statement, and ensuring that changes to scope are approved and managed effectively.

Communicate and collaborate with team members: This includes involving team members in the scope management process, and ensuring that they understand their roles and responsibilities in managing scope.

Use tools and techniques for scope management: This includes using tools such as a Work Breakdown Structure (WBS) to organize and manage scope, and techniques such as Earned Value Management (EVM) to track and measure progress.

In addition to developing the above skills, it is also important to apply them in a professional setting. This includes being able to identify, assess, and control the scope of a project or organization to ensure that it meets its goals and objectives. By developing and implementing effective scope management practices, you can become a valuable asset to your organization and advance in your career as an engineering manager.

XIV
Priority Management

Priority management is the process of identifying, assessing, and managing the priorities of an engineering project or organization. In this chapter, we will explore the importance of priority management in engineering management and provide tips for developing and implementing effective priority management practices in the engineering industry.

The importance of priority management in engineering management lies in the ability to identify and manage the priorities of a project or organization to ensure that it meets its goals and objectives. This includes understanding the types of priorities that are relevant to the engineering industry, such as technical priorities, organizational priorities, and process priorities. Additionally, engineering managers must be able to assess the impact of changes to priorities and implement strategies to ensure that priorities are effectively managed.

Effective priority management in the engineering industry requires a combination of technical, business, and leadership skills. Technical skills include knowledge of engineering principles and practices, as well as problem-solving techniques. Business skills include knowledge of finance, accounting, and project management. Leadership skills include the ability to inspire and motivate teams, make difficult decisions, and resolve problems.

To develop and implement effective priority management practices in the engineering industry, it is important to:

Understand the types of priorities that are relevant to the engineering industry: This includes understanding the different types of priorities, such as technical priorities, organizational priorities, and process priorities.

Develop a priority management plan: This includes outlining the procedures and processes for managing priorities, and assigning roles and responsibilities for priority management.

Continuously monitor and adjust priorities: This includes regularly reviewing and updating the priority management plan, and ensuring that changes to priorities are approved and managed effectively.

Communicate and collaborate with team members: This includes involving team members in the priority management process, and ensuring that they understand their roles and responsibilities in managing priorities.

Use tools and techniques for priority management: This includes using tools such as a priority matrix to organize and manage priorities, and techniques such as critical path analysis to identify and manage critical tasks.

Prioritize and balance competing priorities: This includes balancing competing priorities and ensuring that the most critical tasks and objectives are addressed first.

In addition to developing the above skills, it is also important to apply them in a professional setting. This includes being able to identify, assess, and manage the priorities of a project or organization to ensure that it meets its goals and objectives. By developing and implementing effective priority management practices, you can become a valuable asset to your organization and advance in your career as an engineering manager.

XV

Problem Solving and Decision Making

Problem solving and decision making are critical skills for engineering managers, as they involve identifying and addressing issues that arise during the course of a project or within an organization. In this chapter, we will explore the role of problem solving and decision making in engineering management and provide tips for effective problem solving and decision making in the engineering industry.

The role of problem solving and decision making in engineering management is to provide a framework for addressing issues that arise during the course of a project or within an organization. This includes identifying problems, analyzing data and information, and developing and implementing solutions. Engineering managers must also be able to make decisions that are in the best interest of the organization and its stakeholders.

Effective problem solving and decision making in the engineering industry requires a combination of technical, business, and leadership skills. Technical skills include knowledge of engineering principles and practices, as well as problem-solving techniques such as root cause analysis and design of experiments. Business skills include knowledge of project management methodologies and decision-making frameworks. Leadership skills include the ability to inspire and motivate teams, make difficult decisions, and resolve problems.

To be an effective problem solver and decision maker in the engineering industry, it is important to develop the following skills:

Root cause analysis: To effectively identify and address problems, you must be able to perform root cause analysis. This includes identifying the underlying causes of problems, as well as developing and implementing solutions.

Critical thinking: As an engineering manager, you must be able to analyze data and information, identify patterns and trends, and make informed decisions.

Creativity: To be an effective problem solver, you must be able to think outside of the box and generate new and innovative solutions.

Risk management: As an engineering manager, you must be able to anticipate and manage risks associated with problems and decisions. This includes identifying potential problems, developing strategies to mitigate risks, and monitoring progress.

Communication: To effectively solve problems and make decisions, you must be able to communicate effectively with the project team, stakeholders, and customers. This includes being able to present complex technical information in a way that is easy to understand, as well as being able to listen actively and respond to feedback.

In addition to developing the above skills, it is also important to apply them in a professional setting. This includes being able to identify and address problems and make informed decisions, communicate effectively with the project team, stakeholders, and customers, and manage risk. Additionally, you must be able to build relationships with customers and other stakeholders, negotiate and persuade others to support your ideas and decisions.

It is also essential to stay current with new technologies and industry developments related to problem-solving and decision-making. This can be achieved through continuous learning, such as taking online courses, attending conferences and workshops, and reading industry publications. Additionally, networking with other engineering managers and industry professionals can provide valuable opportunities to learn from others and build relationships.

In conclusion, problem solving and decision making are critical skills for engineering managers. They involve identifying and addressing issues that arise during the course of a project or within an organization. To be an effective problem solver and decision maker in the engineering industry, it is important to develop skills such as root cause analysis, critical thinking, creativity, risk management, and communication. Additionally, it is essential to apply these skills in a professional setting, stay current with new technologies and industry developments, and network with other engineering managers and industry professionals. By investing in your problem-solving and decision-making skills, you can ensure the success of your engineering projects and organization.

XVI

Time Management and Prioritization

Time management and prioritization are essential skills for engineering managers, as they involve effectively managing the time and resources of the project team to ensure that projects are completed on time and within budget. In this chapter, we will explore the importance of time management and prioritization in engineering management and provide tips for effective time management and prioritization in the engineering industry.

The importance of time management and prioritization in engineering management lies in the ability to effectively manage the time and resources of the project team. This includes setting clear deadlines, creating project schedules, and identifying and managing risks. Additionally, engineering managers must be able to prioritize tasks and activities based on their importance and urgency, to ensure that the most critical tasks are completed first.

Effective time management and prioritization in the engineering industry require a combination of technical, business, and leadership skills. Technical skills include knowledge of project management methodologies, such as Agile and Scrum, as well as programming languages and tools. Business skills include knowledge of budgeting, forecasting, and financial management. Leadership skills include the ability to inspire and motivate teams, make difficult decisions, and resolve problems.

To be an effective time manager and prioritizer in the engineering industry, it is important to develop the following skills:

Goal setting: To effectively manage time and resources, you must be able to set clear and realistic goals for the project team. This includes setting deadlines, creating project schedules, and identifying and managing risks.

Prioritization: As an engineering manager, you must be able to prioritize tasks and activities based on their importance and urgency. This includes identifying the most critical tasks and ensuring that they are completed first.

Time management: To effectively manage time and resources, you must be able to manage your time effectively and meet deadlines. This includes setting priorities, delegating tasks, and monitoring progress.

Risk management: As an engineering manager, you must be able to anticipate and manage risks associated with time and resource management. This includes identifying potential problems, developing strategies to mitigate risks, and monitoring progress.

Communication: To effectively manage time and resources, you must be able to communicate effectively with the project team, stakeholders, and customers. This includes being able to present complex technical information in a way that is easy to understand, as well as being able to listen actively and respond to feedback.

In addition to developing the above skills, it is also important to apply them in a professional setting. This includes being able to effectively manage the time and resources of the project team, communicate effectively with the project team, stakeholders, and customers, and make informed decisions. Additionally, you must be able to build relationships with customers and other stakeholders, negotiate and persuade others to support your ideas and decisions, and manage conflict and resolve problems.

It is also essential to stay current with new technologies and industry developments related to time management and prioritization. This can be achieved through continuous learning, such as taking online courses, attending conferences and workshops, and reading industry publications. Additionally, networking with other engineering managers and industry professionals can provide valuable opportunities to learn from others and build relationships.

In conclusion, time management and prioritization are essential skills for engineering managers. They involve effectively managing the time and resources of the project team to ensure that projects are completed on time and within budget. To be an effective time manager and prioritizer in the engineering industry, it is important to develop skills such as, it is important to develop skills such as goal setting, prioritization, time management, risk management, and communication. Additionally, it is essential to apply these skills in a professional setting, stay current with new technologies and industry developments, and network with other engineering managers and industry professionals. By investing in your time management and prioritization skills, you can ensure that your projects are completed on time, within budget, and to the required quality standards. This will ultimately lead to the success of your engineering projects and organization.

• 47 •

XVII

Mentorship and Networking

Mentorship and networking are critical skills for engineering managers, as they involve building relationships and learning from experienced professionals in the industry. In this chapter, we will explore the importance of mentorship and networking in engineering management and provide tips for finding and building mentorship and networking relationships in the engineering industry.

The importance of mentorship and networking in engineering management lies in the ability to learn from experienced professionals in the industry. A mentor can provide guidance, advice, and support, as well as open doors to new opportunities and connections. Networking allows engineering managers to build relationships with industry professionals, learn about new technologies and industry developments, and gain access to new job opportunities.

Effective mentorship and networking in the engineering industry require a combination of technical, business, and leadership skills. Technical skills include knowledge of engineering principles and practices, as well as problem-solving techniques. Business skills include knowledge of project management methodologies and decision-making frameworks. Leadership skills include the ability to inspire and motivate teams, make difficult decisions, and resolve problems.

To be an effective mentee and networker in the engineering industry, it is important to develop the following skills:

Relationship building: To effectively build mentorship and networking relationships, you must be able to build trust and develop positive relationships with industry professionals.

Communication: As an engineering manager, you must be able to communicate effectively with mentors and industry professionals. This includes being able to present complex technical information in a way that is easy to understand, as well as being able to listen actively and respond to feedback.

Networking: To be an effective networker, you must be able to effectively navigate professional networking events and online networking platforms.

Active listening: To effectively learn from mentors and industry professionals, you must be able to actively listen and take in the information they provide.

Professionalism: To effectively build mentorship and networking relationships, you must be able to maintain a high level of professionalism in all interactions.

In addition to developing the above skills, it is also important to apply them in a professional setting. This includes being able to find and build mentorship and networking relationships, communicate effectively with mentors and industry professionals, and navigate professional networking events and online networking platforms. Additionally, you must be able to maintain a high level of professionalism in all interactions and actively listen to the advice and guidance provided by mentors and industry professionals.

One way to find and build mentorship and networking relationships in the engineering industry is to attend industry events, such as conferences and workshops. These events provide opportunities to meet and connect with other professionals in the industry. Additionally, joining professional organizations and joining online networking platforms can also provide valuable opportunities to connect with mentors and industry professionals.

Another way to build mentorship and networking relationships is to seek out mentors within your organization. This can include reaching out to more experienced colleagues or managers, and asking if they would be willing to mentor you. Additionally, you can also seek out mentorship opportunities through mentorship programs offered by professional organizations or industry associations.

Once mentorship and networking relationships have been established, it is important to maintain and nurture them. This includes regularly keeping in touch with mentors and industry professionals, and actively seeking out and responding to opportunities for mentorship and networking. Additionally, it is important to express gratitude and appreciation for the advice and guidance provided by mentors and industry professionals.

In conclusion, mentorship and networking are critical skills for engineering managers. They involve building relationships and learning from experienced professionals in the industry. To be an effective mentee and networker in the engineering industry, it is important to develop skills such as relationship building, communication, networking, active listening, and professionalism. Additionally, it is essential to attend industry events, join professional organizations and online networking platforms, and seek out and maintain mentorship and networking relationships. By investing in your mentorship and networking skills, you can gain valuable insights and opportunities to advance in your career and the industry.

XVIII

Learning and Development

Learning and development is a critical aspect of engineering management, as it enables managers to stay current with the latest trends and technologies in the industry. In this chapter, we will explore the importance of learning and development in engineering management and provide tips for developing and implementing effective learning and development programs in the engineering industry.

The importance of learning and development in engineering management lies in the ability to stay current with the latest trends and technologies in the industry. This includes understanding the types of learning and development that are relevant to the engineering industry, such as technical training, leadership development, and professional development. Additionally, engineering managers must be able to assess the impact of learning and development programs and implement strategies to ensure they are successfully implemented.

Effective learning and development in the engineering industry requires a combination of technical, business, and leadership skills. Technical skills include knowledge of engineering principles and practices, as well as problem-solving techniques. Business skills include knowledge of finance, accounting, and project management. Leadership skills include the ability to inspire and motivate teams, make difficult decisions, and resolve problems.

To develop and implement effective learning and development programs in the engineering industry, it is important to:

Understand the types of learning and development that are relevant to the engineering industry: This includes understanding the different types of learning and development, such as technical training, leadership development, and professional development.

Assess the impact of learning and development programs: This includes using data and metrics to assess the impact of learning and development programs and prioritizing them based on their potential impact.

Implement strategies to ensure learning and development programs are successfully implemented: This includes developing learning and development plans and contingencies and involving stakeholders in the learning and development process.

Regularly review and update learning and development programs: This includes regularly reviewing and updating learning and development programs to ensure they are current and effective, and incorporating lessons learned from previous programs.

Communicate and collaborate with team members: This includes involving team members in the learning and development process and ensuring that they understand their roles and responsibilities in learning and development.

Provide opportunities for self-directed learning: This includes encouraging and supporting team members to take initiative in their own learning and development, and providing resources such as books, articles, and online tutorials.

In addition to developing the above skills, it is also important to apply them in a professional setting. This includes being able to identify, assess, and implement learning and development programs that will improve the performance of a project or organization. By developing and implementing effective learning and development programs, you can become a valuable asset to your organization and advance in your career as an engineering manager.

XIX

Performance management

Performance management is a critical aspect of engineering management, as it enables managers to effectively evaluate and improve the performance of their team members. In this chapter, we will explore the importance of performance management in engineering management and provide tips for developing and implementing effective performance management practices in the engineering industry.

The importance of performance management in engineering management lies in the ability to evaluate and improve the performance of team members. This includes understanding the types of performance that are relevant to the engineering industry, such as technical performance, organizational performance, and process performance. Additionally, engineering managers must be able to assess the impact of performance management practices and implement strategies to ensure they are successfully implemented.

Effective performance management in the engineering industry requires a combination of technical, business, and leadership skills. Technical skills include knowledge of engineering principles and practices, as well as problem-solving techniques. Business skills include knowledge of finance, accounting, and project management. Leadership skills include the ability to inspire and motivate teams, make difficult decisions, and resolve problems.

To develop and implement effective performance management practices in the engineering industry, it is important to:

Understand the types of performance that are relevant to the engineering industry: This includes understanding the different types of performance, such as technical performance, organizational performance, and process performance.

Assess the impact of performance management practices: This includes using data and metrics to assess the impact of performance management practices, and prioritizing them based on their potential impact.

Implement strategies to ensure performance management practices are successfully implemented: This includes developing performance management plans and contingencies, and involving stakeholders in the performance management process.

Regularly review and update performance management practices: This includes regularly reviewing and updating performance management practices to ensure they are current and effective, and incorporating lessons learned from previous projects.

Communicate and collaborate with team members: This includes involving team members in the performance management process, and ensuring that they understand their roles and responsibilities in performance management.

Provide regular feedback and coaching: This includes providing regular feedback and coaching to team members to help them improve their performance.

In addition to developing the above skills, it is also important to apply them in a professional setting. This includes being able to evaluate and improve the performance of team members to ensure that a project or organization meets its goals and objectives. By developing and implementing effective performance management practices, you can become a valuable asset to your organization and advance in your career as an engineering manager.

XX

Appraisal management

Team appraisal management is a critical aspect of engineering management, as it enables managers to effectively evaluate the performance of their teams. In this chapter, we will explore the importance of team appraisal management in engineering management and provide tips for developing and implementing effective team appraisal practices in the engineering industry.

The importance of team appraisal management in engineering management lies in the ability to evaluate the performance of teams as a whole. This includes understanding the types of team appraisals that are relevant to the engineering industry, such as technical team appraisals, organizational team appraisals, and process team appraisals. Additionally, engineering managers must be able to assess the impact of team appraisal practices and implement strategies to ensure they are successfully implemented.

Effective team appraisal management in the engineering industry requires a combination of technical, business, and leadership skills. Technical skills include knowledge of engineering principles and practices, as well as problem-solving techniques. Business skills include knowledge of finance, accounting, and project management. Leadership skills include the ability to inspire and motivate teams, make difficult decisions, and resolve problems.

To develop and implement effective team appraisal practices in the engineering industry, it is important to:

Understand the types of team appraisals that are relevant to the engineering industry: This includes understanding the different types of team appraisals, such as technical team appraisals, organizational team appraisals, and process team appraisals.

Assess the impact of team appraisal practices: This includes using data and metrics to assess the impact of team appraisal practices, and prioritizing them based on their potential impact.

Implement strategies to ensure team appraisal practices are successfully implemented: This includes developing team appraisal plans and contingencies, and involving stakeholders in the team appraisal process.

Regularly review and update team appraisal practices: This includes regularly reviewing and updating team appraisal practices to ensure they are current and effective, and incorporating lessons learned from previous projects.

Communicate and collaborate with team members: This includes involving team members in the team appraisal process, and ensuring that they understand their roles and responsibilities in team appraisal.

Use tools and techniques for team appraisal: This includes using tools such as a team appraisal matrix to organize and manage team appraisals, and techniques such as 360-degree feedback to gather input from multiple perspectives.

In addition to developing the above skills, it is also important to apply them in a professional setting. This includes being able to evaluate the performance of teams to ensure that a project or organization meets its goals and objectives. By developing and implementing effective team appraisal practices, you can become a valuable asset to your organization and advance in your career as an engineering manager.

XXI

Conflict handelling

Team conflict is an inevitable part of any team or organization, and it is important for engineering managers to be able to effectively handle and resolve conflicts within their teams. In this chapter, we will explore the importance of team conflict handling in engineering management and provide tips for developing and implementing effective conflict management strategies in the engineering industry.

The importance of team conflict handling in engineering management lies in the ability to maintain a positive and productive team environment. Conflicts can arise due to a variety of factors, such as personality clashes, competing priorities, and communication breakdowns. It is the responsibility of the engineering manager to identify and address conflicts in a timely and effective manner.

Effective team conflict handling in the engineering industry requires a combination of technical, business, and leadership skills. Technical skills include knowledge of engineering principles and practices, as well as problem-solving techniques. Business skills include knowledge of finance, accounting, and project management. Leadership skills include the ability to inspire and motivate teams, make difficult decisions, and resolve problems.

To develop and implement effective team conflict handling strategies in the engineering industry, it is important to:

Understand the types of conflicts that may arise within a team: This includes understanding the different types of conflicts, such as personality conflicts, task conflicts, and communication conflicts.

Assess the impact of conflicts on the team: This includes using data and metrics to assess the impact of conflicts on the team, and prioritizing them based on their potential impact.

Implement strategies to resolve conflicts effectively: This includes developing conflict management plans and contingencies, and involving stakeholders in the conflict management process.

Regularly review and update conflict management strategies: This includes regularly reviewing and updating conflict management strategies to ensure they are current and effective, and incorporating lessons learned from previous conflicts.

Communicate and collaborate with team members: This includes involving team members in the conflict management process, and ensuring that they understand their roles and responsibilities in conflict management.

Use tools and techniques for conflict management: This includes using tools such as a conflict resolution matrix to organize and manage conflicts, and techniques such as mediation and negotiation to resolve conflicts.

Developing empathy and emotional intelligence: This includes being able to understand and relate to the emotions and perspectives of others, and using this understanding to effectively resolve conflicts.

In addition to developing the above skills, it is also important to apply them in a professional setting. This includes being able to handle and resolve conflicts within a team to ensure that a project or organization meets its goals and objectives. By developing and implementing effective team conflict handling strategies, you can become a valuable asset to your organization and advance in your career as an engineering manager.

XXII

Deal with Empathy

Empathy is an essential skill for any leader, and it is especially important for engineering managers to be able to understand and relate to the emotions and perspectives of their team members. In this chapter, we will explore the importance of empathy in engineering management and provide tips for developing and implementing effective empathy strategies in the engineering industry.

The importance of empathy in engineering management lies in the ability to create a positive and productive team environment. Empathy allows engineering managers to understand the perspectives and emotions of their team members, which in turn enables them to make better decisions and resolve conflicts more effectively. It also helps in building trust, fostering collaboration and motivation, and promoting engagement and commitment among team members.

Effective empathy in the engineering industry requires a combination of technical, business, and leadership skills. Technical skills include knowledge of engineering principles and practices, as well as problem-solving techniques. Business skills include knowledge of finance, accounting, and project management. Leadership skills include the ability to inspire and motivate teams, make difficult decisions, and resolve problems.

To develop and implement effective empathy strategies in the engineering industry, it is important to:

Understand the importance of empathy in engineering management: This includes understanding the benefits of empathy in creating a positive team environment, and how it can improve decision making and conflict resolution.

Assess the level of empathy within the team: This includes using data and metrics to assess the level of empathy within the team, and identifying areas for improvement.

Implement strategies to develop empathy within the team: This includes developing empathy training programs, and involving stakeholders in the empathy development process.

Regularly review and update empathy strategies: This includes regularly reviewing and updating empathy strategies to ensure they are current and effective, and incorporating lessons learned from previous experiences.

Communicate and collaborate with team members: This includes involving team members in the empathy development process, and ensuring that they understand their roles and responsibilities in empathy.

Use tools and techniques for empathy development: This includes using tools such as empathy maps, role-playing exercises, and active listening techniques to develop empathy within the team.

Practice mindfulness and self-awareness: This includes being aware of one's own thoughts, emotions, and actions, and how they affect others.

In addition to developing the above skills, it is also important to apply them in a professional setting. This includes being able to understand and relate to the emotions and perspectives of others, and using this understanding to make better decisions and resolve conflicts more effectively. By developing and implementing effective empathy strategies, you can become a valuable asset to your organization and advance in your career as an engineering manager.

Conclusion

In this book, we have explored the various aspects of engineering management and the skills that are necessary to be a successful engineering manager. We have covered topics such as understanding the software engineering industry, developing technical skills, leadership and communication, software project management, financial management, problem solving and decision making, time management and prioritization, mentorship and networking, business acumen, technical acumen, people growth, process management, risk management, change management, scope management, priority management, learning and development, people/team performance management, team appraisal management, team conflict handling and dealing with empathy.

As an engineering manager, it is important to have a strong understanding of the industry and the technical skills necessary to lead and manage teams. Additionally, it is important to have strong leadership and communication skills, as well as knowledge of project management, finance, and problem-solving. Empathy and emotional intelligence also play a critical role in effective leadership and management.

It is also important to understand the importance of mentorship and networking in the engineering industry, and to take advantage of opportunities to learn from more experienced professionals.

In conclusion, becoming an engineering manager requires a diverse set of skills and knowledge, and the ability to apply them in a professional setting. It is a challenging but rewarding career path, and by developing and implementing the skills discussed in this book, you can become a valuable asset to your organization and advance in your career as an engineering manager.

Glossary

A glossary of key terms and concepts used in the book is provided for easy reference. This will assist readers in understanding the technical language used in the book.

Acumen: A keen understanding and ability to make good judgments and quick decisions.

Business Acumen: A keen understanding of business principles and the ability to apply them effectively.

Change Management: The process of managing changes in an organization, including the implementation and communication of changes to stakeholders.

Conflict Management: The process of identifying, addressing, and resolving conflicts within a team or organization.

Decision Making: The process of making choices among a set of options based on the available information.

Empathy: The ability to understand and share the feelings of others.

Engineering Management: The application of management principles to the planning, design, construction, and maintenance of engineering projects.

Financial Management: The process of managing the financial resources of an organization, including budgeting, forecasting, and financial analysis.

Leadership: The ability to guide and inspire others to achieve a common goal.

Mentorship: A relationship in which a more experienced or knowledgeable person guides and advises a less experienced or knowledgeable person.

Networking: The process of building and maintaining relationships with other people in order to achieve a common goal.

People Growth: The process of developing the skills and abilities of individuals within an organization.

Performance Management: The process of evaluating and improving the performance of individuals within an organization.

Problem Solving: The process of identifying, analyzing, and solving problems.

Process Management: The process of managing and improving the processes within an organization.

Project Management: The process of planning, organizing, and managing resources to achieve a specific goal or objective.

Risk Management: The process of identifying, assessing, and mitigating risks in an organization.

Scope Management: The process of defining and controlling the scope of a project, including the goals, objectives, deliverables, and requirements.

Technical Acumen: A keen understanding of technical principles and the ability to apply them effectively.

Time Management: The process of organizing and planning the use of time in order to achieve specific goals or objectives.

Prioritization: The process of determining the order of importance or urgency of tasks or activities.

References

A list of references used in the book is provided for further reading and research. This includes books, articles, and websites that provide additional information and insights on the topics discussed in the book.

"Project Management for Engineering and Construction" by Garold D. Oberlender

"Leadership and Communication in Engineering" by John A. Clements

"Financial Management for Engineers" by John A. White

"Risk Management for Engineers" by John A. White

"The Art of Problem Solving" by George Polya

"The One Minute Manager" by Ken Blanchard and Spencer Johnson

"The 7 Habits of Highly Effective People" by Stephen Covey

"The Power of Emotional Intelligence" by Daniel Goleman

"People Management for Engineers" by John A. White

"The Lean Startup" by Eric Ries

These references provide additional information and insights on the topics discussed in the book, and we recommend them for further reading and research.

About The Author

Meet Sumon Mal, a seasoned engineering manager and sought-after expert in the field. With over 12 years of experience in software engineering and a Masters in Computer Applications, Sumon brings a wealth of knowledge and practical experience to his writing. He has a passion for sharing his insights on engineering management with others, and has written several books, including "Smart Communication" and "SDLC: A Must-Known Fact for Engineering Managers".

Sumon is a thought leader in the engineering management space, regularly speaking at industry conferences and sharing his expertise through articles and books. He has a deep understanding of the key concepts and skills necessary for success in this field, and is dedicated to helping others achieve their full potential as engineering managers.

If you're looking to take your engineering management skills to the next level, look no further than Sumon Mal. With clear, concise writing and a focus on real-world applications, Sumon's books are an essential resource for anyone looking to excel in this field. Reach out to him at sumonmal009@gmail.com for further assistance or to provide feedback on his work. To learn more about Sumon's professional background, check out his LinkedIn profile at https://www.linkedin.com/in/sumonmal/

Thank You Note

I would like to express my gratitude to you for taking the time to read this book. I hope that it has provided valuable insights and practical tips for success in the field of engineering management. I am confident that the concepts and skills discussed in this book will help you to become a more effective engineering manager and make a positive impact in your field.

I would like to thank the reviewers who have helped to improve this book and make it as valuable as possible.

I would also like to thank the publisher for their support and for making this book a reality.

Thank you again for your support and I wish you all the best in your engineering management journey.

Sumon Mal

www.ingramcontent.com/pod-product-compliance
Lightning Source LLC
Chambersburg PA
CBHW052118150726
48002CB00006B/2400